Eternal Bonds

A Journey Through Love, Parenthood, and Legacy

Sairam Tadepalli

BookLeaf Publishing

India | USA | UK

Copyright © Sairam Tadepalli
All Rights Reserved.

This book has been self-published with all reasonable efforts taken to make the material error-free by the author. No part of this book shall be used, reproduced in any manner whatsoever without written permission from the author, except in the case of brief quotations embodied in critical articles and reviews.

The Author of this book is solely responsible and liable for its content including but not limited to the views, representations, descriptions, statements, information, opinions, and references ["Content"]. The Content of this book shall not constitute or be construed or deemed to reflect the opinion or expression of the Publisher or Editor. Neither the Publisher nor Editor endorse or approve the Content of this book or guarantee the reliability, accuracy, or completeness of the Content published herein and do not make any representations or warranties of any kind, express or implied, including but not limited to the implied warranties of merchantability, fitness for a particular purpose.

The Publisher and Editor shall not be liable whatsoever...

Made with ❤ on the BookLeaf Publishing Platform

www.bookleafpub.in

www.bookleafpub.com

To All the Parents of the World,

This book is a humble tribute to the love, sacrifices, and strength that define you. You are the unsung heroes behind countless stories, unwavering pillars in times of turmoil, and the gentle whispers of encouragement to follow our dreams.

Thank you for the sleepless nights when you calmed our cries g, for the hands that directed our first steps, and for the broken hearts that felt our victories and failures as one. Your love is so pure and everlasting that not even a million words can measure it.

You have taught us that fatherhood is not merely an identity; it is a powerful pilgrimage of selflessness and struggle for the well-being of another. In your hugs, words of encouragement, and lessons you have imparted, these gifts shape futures and build legacies.

This one is for you, for your infinite patience, your silent strength, and your limitless love. It is a tribute to the innumerable moments, large and small, that make the tale of parenthood one of the most beautiful stories ever told.

May these poems resonate with your emotions, honor your struggles, and remind you of the profound impact you have on this world.

With all my heart, I thank you for your love and sacrifices and for being the guiding lights generations. This book is my way of saying: We see you. We appreciate you. We are forever grateful for you.

With deepest respect and love,

Sairam Tadepalli

Acknowledgement

To my loving parents, whose love and guidance have shaped me, and to all the parents and well-wishers worldwide—thank you for your unwavering love and sacrifice.

This book is but a small homage to your strength, love, and the legacy you build.

Preface

Eternal Bonds is a heartfelt collection of 42 poems that beautifully captures the transformative journey of parenthood and the eternal love that ties families together. Through tender verses and poignant imagery, this book unfolds the stages of life, from the anticipation of becoming parents to the bittersweet moments of letting children carve their paths, while reflecting on the enduring legacy of love passed through generations.

Each poem delves into universal themes of joy, sacrifice, pride, and resilience, resonating deeply with readers as they navigate the highs and lows of life. From the first cry of a newborn to the milestones of childhood, from the turbulence of adolescence to the triumphs of adulthood, and finally, to the reflective moments of aging and legacy—this anthology is a tribute to love's evolution, a bond that transcends time and space.

Key Themes:

The Miracle of Life: This book captures the emotions of becoming parents and the joy of witnessing a child's firsts.

Unconditional Love: Highlighting the depth of parental love expressed through sacrifice, guidance, and nurturing.

Growth and Transformation: This section explores a child's journey to become an independent adult while parents learn to let go.

Challenges and Resilience: Navigating life's struggles with unwavering support and strength.

Legacy and Reflection: Celebrating the eternal bonds that shape future generations.

Why This Book Matters:

In a world where fleeting connections dominate, *Eternal Bonds* is a timeless reminder of the enduring power of familial love. It celebrates the everyday moments that shape our lives and the extraordinary emotions that connect us all.
This anthology is perfect for parents, children, and anyone seeking to reflect on the beauty of human relationships. It's a book to cherish, share, and pass down as a legacy of love.

The Joy of Discovering Parenthood

The Joy of Finding Parenthood

A mere murmur of a wondrous abstraction,

A fleeting moment, yet eternity delivered.

An unseen future, an uncharted love,

This sows a seed of joy in our hearts.

Eve, it seems, the world is fairer, the skies cleaner,

As dreams of you grow ever near.

A fresh chapter, a road not taken,

A prayer sustains the life we've lived.

A Mother's Initial Emotions

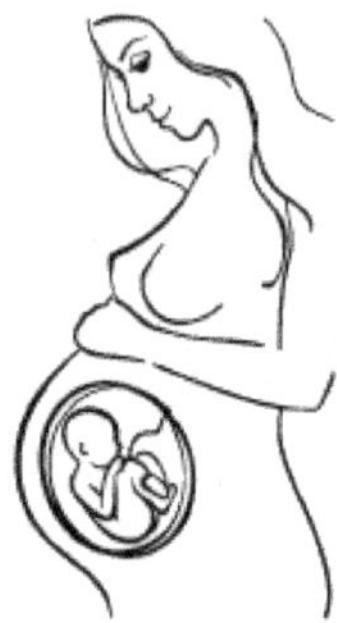

A gentle sigh, a touch of recognition,
A precious gift, a miracle waiting to be born.
Inside my body, a life begins to stir,
It is a process filled with love, a triumph of creation.
In the stillness, I stand in silence, looking up,
For brightness and contentment to lead me forward.
Although I have not beheld your face yet,
You already dwell within my soul.

A Father's Dreams for the Unborn Child

I imagine your laughter, your delicate hands,
A life of wonder as the world expands.
Through every thought, I dream anew of all
the things I'll teach you.
A protector, a guide, I'll always stay,
Your dreams and hopes won't fade away.
I promise you, my little star,
You'll know how loved you indeed are.

The Mother's Bond with the Baby in Her Womb

A quiet rhythm, a melody so sweet,
Your tiny heartbeat, our hearts now meet.
I feel your kicks, your growing might,
A bong so strong, a love so bright.

You're my secret, my quiet surprise,
A miracle unseen by others' eyes.
I carry you close, my heart aglow,
A love so deep, only we know.

The Father's Anticipation of Meeting the Baby

I count the days, each moment slow,
Awaiting the time when love will show.
The little one I yearn to see,
A part of you, a part of me.

With every day, my heart expands,
Dreaming of holding your tiny hands.
Oh, how I long for that first embrace,
The day I finally see your face.

Preparing for the Baby's Arrival

We paint the room, we tuck away clothes,
Tiny blankets, soft as petals on a rose.
Every detail, tended with care,
A world of love we're building there.

A cradle placed, a lullaby sung,
The waiting heart, with love, has burned.
Each moment spent preparing for you,
Our hearts alight, our dreams renewed.

The Mother's Pain and Courage During Delivery

Waves of pain, a stormy sea,
A battle fought to see you free.
Each scream, each cry, a step toward grace,
For you, my love, I'll find my place.

Through tears and strength, I bring you near,
Your first soft cry, the sound I hold dear.
Through pain, I found a joy so enormous,
Finally, the time you've been waiting for.

The First Cry of the Baby

A sharp, quivering sound, both fragile and strong,
A moment where we are no longer alone.
Your cry declares, "I'm here,"
Filling our hearts with joy sincere.

That tiny voice, so fierce, so new,
A song of a miracles, one that's come true.
In that cry, the world stood still,
A love awakened eternal in will.

Parents' Overwhelming Emotions at First Sight

Tiny fingers, a wrinkled face,
A moment suspended in timeless space.
Eyes that meet, a silent vow,
A bond unbroken, beginning now.

Our hearts overflow, too full to speak,
Tears cascade down each cheek.
In your presence, the world is whole,
You've filled that void within our soul.

Naming the Baby and Its Deeper Meaning

A name so sweet, a gift we choose,
A word imbued with dreams we muse.
Each letter sings its own soft tune,
A symbol of all you'll one day bloom.

With care, we ponder; with love, we weave,
A legacy for you to receive.
Your name will resound through the years,
A beacon of pride through joy and tears.

Watching the Baby's First Smile

It forms a little arc, but it nevertheless
illuminates the room,
A loving light chases away all darkness.
Your first smile, oh, what a rarity,
It was a moment of unadulterated joy.

And a sign of love, a bond profound
and new,
A present from the cosmos that I am sharing
with you.
Each smile you (own) is a (gold) piece,
It is a story of joy, told beautifully.

Celebrating the Baby's First Word

One quiet note, a minuscule beginning,
A bare utterance that gets our attention.
"Mama" or "Papa," it makes no difference,
Our happiness now knows no bounds but our
pitter-patter.

Your voice is a whisper yet still assertive and
loud,
It has the power to endow and fill the days.
Now, as each letter is spoken, we achieve
another status,
This is where each second stands still.

The Wonder of the Baby's First Crawl

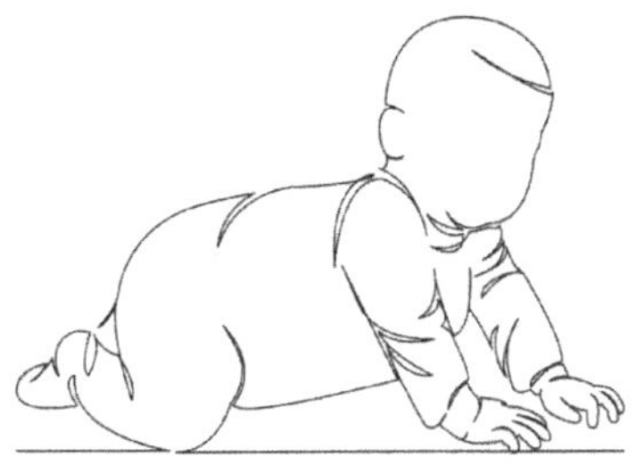

Gripped by envy, across the floor you stray,
Where you don't know, curiosity paves the
way.
Your little fingers and knees crawl,
A new horizon, the world's wide door.

We cheer for you, our little star,
In awe of how brave you already are.
With each little step you take, our hearts take
flight,
You are our joy, our guiding light.

The Joy of the Baby's First Steps

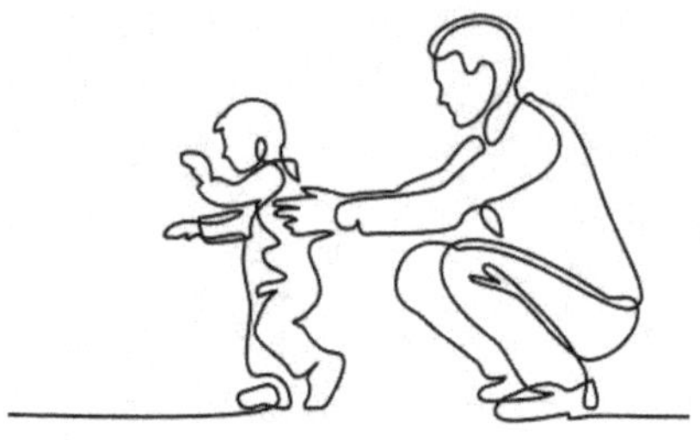

Jittery legs, a bobbling posture,
It is a bold step, a fresh opportunity.
Here to direct, arms open wide,
Proudly walking forward;

Each step you take, a moment divine,
A memory cherished, forever mine.
We clap, we laugh, we shout with glee,
For you, the first step is history.

Seeing the baby's Personality Emerge

A sparkle ignites within your curious eyes,
A fearless heart, where wonders lie.
With every giggle, every sign,
Your unique self begins to crown.

Your quirks, your charms, your little ways,
Bring endless wonder to our days.
We see the person you're meant to be,
A masterpiece of destiny.

Watching the Child Play and Explore the World

In fields of green, beneath the sun,
We watch you laugh, we watch you run.
A tiny explorer with a curious mind,
In every moment, joy you find.

Through mud-streaked hands and playful
cheer,
You paint the world, your canvas clear.
Your spirit dances, wild and free,
A boundless joy for all to see.

Sending the Child to School for the First Time

A little bag, a tiny hand,
You step away from our hands.
Our hearts ache, our pride does grow,
For now, the world you'll start to know.

We wave goodbye, swallow the tears,
Hoping you'll conquer your fears.
The school bell rings, the door swings wide,
A new adventure waits inside.

Helping with Homework and Guiding Early Learning

Books and pencils, scattered around,
Tiny questions, answers profound.
We sit together, side by side,
Your curious mind is our most incredible
pride.

Through sums and words, we gently steer,
Building knowledge, year by year.
Each lesson taught a bond we grow,
A love for learning starts to show.

Celebrating Childhood Milestones

A toothless grin, a trophy held high,
The first time you dared to touch the sky.
Every milestone, big or small,
We celebrate them; we treasure them all.

Your achievements, your little winds,
Bring joy that endlessly begins.
Each step forward, a tale to tell,
Of how you've grown, of how you've excelled.

Encouraging Dreams and Hobbies

With crayons in hand, you sketch your
dreams,
In every stroke, your passion gleams.
We cheer you on with hearts held high,
For your dreams are ours to amplify.

Through dance, through sport, through songs
you sing,
We see your joy, the art you breathe.
Your passions bloom, your talents flow,
A vibrant world, you start to show.

Navigating Early Struggles with Kindness

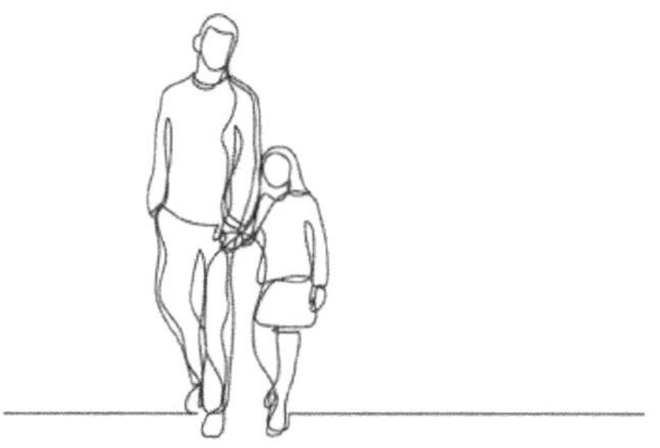

A scraped knee, a math test failed,
Moments where your courage derailed.
We wipe your tears, we lift your chin,
Guiding you back to hope within.

For struggles shape both heart and mind,
In every fall, resilience you'll find.
We'll be your haven, your soft embrace,
As you grow through life at your own pace.

Witnessing Friendships Blossom

Your laughter echoes, pure and sweet,
As tiny hands and hearts do meet.
In games and secrets, bonds and spun,
Friendships forged beneath the sun.

We watch you grow, your world expands,
A circle of love, hand in hand.
Through every giggle, every play,
Your friends light up your every day.

Watching the Child Overcome Fear

A quivering lip, a worried gaze,
Yet courage breaks through the timid haze.
You take a step, you rise once more,
Defying doubt, your spirit soars.

We cheer you on, we see you fight,
A tiny spark becomes your light.
Through each small triumph, fear dies and
fades,
A braver soul, a strength displayed.

Guiding Them Through Life's First Disappointments

The first tear falls, a heart dies ache,
A dream once held begins to break.
We hold you close, we help you see,
That life moves on, as it must be.

Each disappointment, a lesson learned,
A flame of resilience brightly burned.
Through every fall, we help you rise,
Your guiding light, where strength resides.

Pride in the Child's Achievements

A certificate clutched, a medal worn,
In your success, a joy is born.
We clap, we cheer, our hearts take flight,
In your victories, the world feels right.

From spelling bees to pained art,
Your achievements lift our hearts.
You strive, you shine, you light the way,
A beacon bright, day by day.

Navigating Teenage Transformations

A voice that deepens, a growing frame,
A changing soul we can't quite name.
With every step, you pull away,
Yet, in your heart, we hope to stay.

We guide, we listen, we understand,
Though shifting tides, we hold your hand.
For though you change, you're still our own,
A love unyielding, fully grown.

Supporting Their First Independent Choices

You take the lead, you stake your claim,
Decisions forming, unplanned and grand.
With every choice, your voice is heard,
A fledgling soul, a soaring bird.

We stand behind you, we cheer your try,
As you chase dreams, as you reach high.
For in your freedom, we find delight,
Watching you shine, bold and bright.

Emotional Moments During High School Graduation

The cap, the gown, the tassel turned,
A moment where your triumphs burned.
We watch you cross, a proud display,
The end of a chapter, a brand-new way.

Tears of joy, of pride, of love,
A milestone blessed by the stars above.
You've grown so much, a future-wide,
Our hearts swell with parental pride.

Sending the Child Off to College or Work

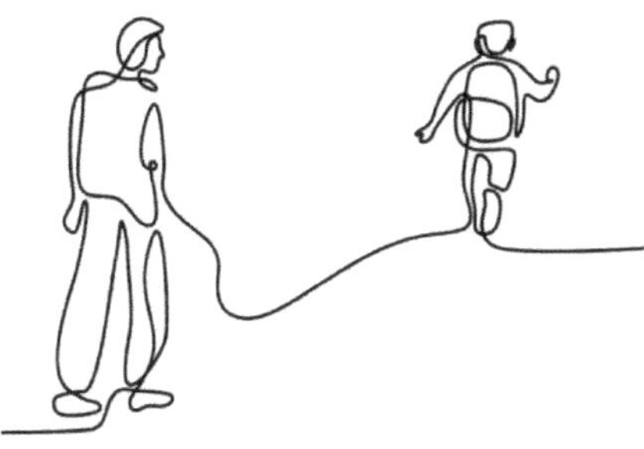

A suitcase packed, a bittersweet goodbye,
Our little bird takes to the sky.
With every step, our pride dies to grow,
Though parting hurts, we let you go.

The nest feels empty, the house so still,
Yet our hearts are complete, our dreams
fulfilled.
For you are ready, strong and wise,
To carve your path beneath life's skies.

The First Big Goodbye

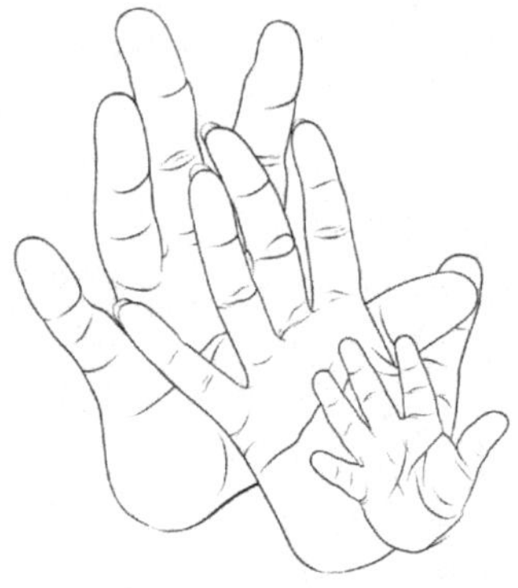

The door swings shut, the silent loud,
Our hearts cling tight, yet we're so proud.
The first goodbye, a bittersweet song,
A moment where you truly belong.

We wave with love, though tears may fall,
For life has answered your heart's call.
Through every goodbye, a hello will bloom,
And love will bridge the miles of room.

Celebrating Their First Career Success

You are sentences woven, layer by layer.
Once more, it is an adventure, a tale told.
You deserve this place, this moment's cheer,
The bright past and the apparent future.

We raise our glass to your strength,
your wishes fulfilled,
You have the world before you.
Our hearts burn like a flame; in each
triumph,
For in your victories, our pride shall shine.

Witnessing Their Love Story Unfold

A glance exchanged, spark alight,
A journey starts, and love takes flight.
We watch you smile, your heart so full,
It is a tale of joy, so beautiful.

With open arms, we welcome them,
A love that shines, a precious gem.
Through your love story, we relive,
The magic that life and heartstrings give.

Embracing a New Family Through Marriage

A union blessed, a bond so true,
A moment shared between us and you.
We stand with pride, with hearts so warm,
As love takes on its rightful form.

Through vows exchanged and lives entwined,
A more fabulous family, hearts aligned.
We gain not just a child anew,
But the joy in knowing they cherish you.

Becoming Grandparents and a New Chapter

A fragile cry, a tiny hand,
A miracle we hadn't planned.
In you, we see a love reborn,
A brighter day, a golden morning.

Grandparenthood, a joy so sweet,
A love that makes our lives complete.
Through every laugh, through every tear,
A new chapter starts, so bright, so clear.

Watching Them Parent with Pride

You hold their hand, you soothe their cries,
A gentle love reflected in your eyes.
We watch you care; we watch you guide,
With hearts so full, with endless pride.

The lessons learned the love you knew,
Are now the gifts you pass on, too.
To see your parents is a dream come true,
For in their joy, we see you anew.

Reflecting on Their Journey as Adults

We sit in silence, memories flow,
Of tiny steps and how you'd grow.
Now you're strong, with dreams of your own,
A life you've built, a strength well-known.

In your laughter, we see our past,
A love so deep, forever vast.
Through every choice, through every climb,
You've made our lives a work of time.

Sharing Wisdom Through Life's Challenges

When storms arise, and paths grow steep,
We're here to help, your fears to keep.
With every word, with hands outstretched,
We offer strength, a love unmatched.

Life's challenges may bend, not break,
For wisdom grows from each mistake.
Through every trial, through every pain,
We'll guide you home to joy again.

Celebrating Their Milestones as Adults

A house you've had built, a dream fulfilled,
A legacy in which we've believed.
It keeps us standing proud, keeps us
clapping, keeps us cheering,
Your accomplishments bring us joy.

From achievements you've accomplished
to plans you've laid,
Your journey grows, and your path is well
laid.
Your every step, your every star,
The fact that you are here to celebrate the
untold massive grace.

Growing Old Together with Their Support

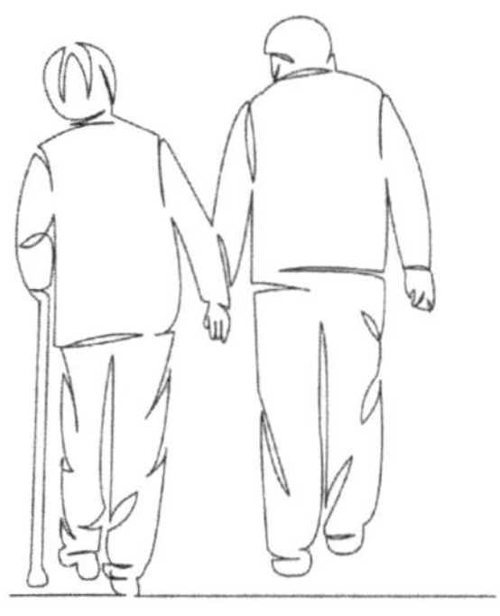

With grey hair and a slowing gait,
We recognise your love and your gentle
grace.
As once we cared for you, you care for us,
A circle closed; a life completed.

Through every laugh, through every tear,
Your warmth still draws us near
The last secret of caretaker is that ageing —
we have peace so true,
For in your case, love redeems.

Leaving a Legacy of Love

One day, when we are but a thought,
The love we shared won't be forgotten.
Through stories told, through hearts, you'll
guide,
Our legacy, in you, abides.

Each hug, each kiss, each whispered word,
Will echo in the lives you've stirred.
Our greatest gift, our brightest star,
It is the love we leave in who we are.